THE DEATHBED PLAYBOY

to whom it may concern —
I hope you find
something here to like —

Phil Dacey

member
West Side Y
5/2010

Also by Philip Dacey

THE
DEATHBED
PLAYBOY

POEMS

BY

PHILIP DACEY

EWU
P·R·E·S·S
Eastern Washington University Press
Cheney, Washington 1999

Cover painting by Thomas Hart Benton (1889-1975)
Persephone, 1938.
The Nelson-Atkins Museum of Art, Kansas City, Missouri
(Purchase: acquired through the Yellow Freight Foundation Art Acquisition Fund
and the generosity of Mrs. Herbert O. Peet, Richard J. Stern, the Doris Jones
Stein Foundation, the Jacob L. and Ella C. Loose Foundation, Mr. and Mrs.
Richard M. Levin, and Mr. and Mrs. Marvin Rich)

Cover and book design by Scott Poole

Library of Congress Cataloging-in-Publication Data
Dacey, Philip
The deathbed playboy : poems / by Philip Dacey
p.   cm.
ISBN 0-910055-47-5 (paper)
ISBN 0-910055-48-3 (cloth)
I. Title.
PS3554.A23D43   1999
811'.54–DC21   99-91706
CIP

CONTENTS

I

II

III

for
Emmett and Barb,
Austin and Camilla,
and Fay,
as they all travel
"in the sweet world where possibilities rule"

THE
DEATHBED
PLAYBOY

I

RECORDED MESSAGE

"Your call is important to us.
Thank you for holding."
— Norwest Banks

Your call is important to us.
That is why, although we are not now answering,
we will, as soon as possible, answer,
provided you keep holding.
If you do not keep holding,
we assure you
we will not answer.

Your call is important to us
because you are holding,
because you are the kind of person who,
when asked to hold, keeps holding,
at least so far.
As difficult as it might be for you to believe,
not everyone holds.
Some stop holding even before we have finished
asking them to hold. Some, we are coming to suspect,
take special pleasure
in not holding.

Lest you begin to doubt us, remember
that if we did not intend to answer,
we would not let you hold,
as you will note we continue to do.
We thank you for holding.
We are thanking you now
so that later, should you have held
long enough for us to answer,
we needn't spend time

thanking you then
for having held.
We know your time is important to you,
as our time is important to us.
Unfortunately, we have none of our own right now
to answer you.

Finally, let us emphasize that
the importance to us of your call
is demonstrated by our
not answering
in this particular way.
In fact, this particular way of not answering —
when considered from the angle
from which we would like you
to consider it —
can be construed
as our way of answering.
We hope our answer, such as it is,
is as important to you
as your call is to us,
so important
that you are now ready
to hear it again.

DIFFICULT CORNERS

1. Introduction to "North Broadway & Grand"

You may have seen my brother on TV,
the traffic cop who dances as he works.
Candid Camera had him doing it
to music, a Baryshnikov in blue
stylishly choreographed by Twyla Tharp.
Years before, that corner had been the worst
for gridlock: nearby factories and trains
and highway entrances and exits tied
travellers (and city planners) in knots.
A million dollar set of lights installed
in place of one patrolman under siege
fizzled, followed again by manpower,
this time three policemen strategically
placed, the corner's own Bermuda Triangle.
Not many problems disappeared in there,
but soon the technocrats threw up their hands
and let the three, my brother one of them,
sink or swim in that sea of honking cars.

This went on until one now fateful day
both of my brother's partners called in sick.
The station chief, fed up, said, "Put Dacey
out there and see what he can do alone,"
expecting nothing. Which was what he got —
no jam, no backup, no cursing drivers,
only autos moving slick as skaters
on new ice, sweet perpetual motion,
the way it was just after World War II,
thanks to my brother's bumps and grinds, his arms
now windmill blades, now darting rapiers.
He never stopped, so why should the traffic?

It was as if he'd waited all his life
for just this moment, backstage, as it were,
the old star finally ill and a new star born.
You've got to understand his years till then
had had their troubles, like too many wives —
I always forget that fourth one's name — but now
he'd come into his own, local celeb,
and soon not so local. A California
film crew documented him in *Pop Cop*
and folks from near and far regularly
came to watch, thus creating more traffic, which
he handled with his usual purposeful
show, and sometimes with a "Move it, Buddy!"
(Sometimes he made them go a way they did
not want to go. But they did flow, did flow.)
Businesses threw banquets for him, and more
than one passing driver's left hand shot out
to pat him on the back "Good job there, Dace!"
And though art meant for him Glenn Miller
period, I swear to see him work you'd think
there had to be a Muse of traffic cops.
As brave bullfighters work close to the horns,
my brother worked close to the cars, too close,
and twice was knocked into the hospital.
Flowers from stranded drivers filled his room
and when he returned, their horns blared welcome
in a steady stream his entire rush hour shift.
The rock was back, mid-channel, the river
swirling happily and noisily around him.
When he retired, they redesigned the streets.
I like to think that since he didn't have
some numbered jersey to hang up, enshrined,
for him they hung up several city blocks.

So when my sister knew she had three months
or less to live and chose to die at home,

my brother, toughest of tough cops, came daily
to his kid sis's place to act as Number One
Nurse, cleaning and feeding her, listening,
and at the very last was holding her,
he the master of difficult passages,
never off-duty, by his sure ways even
leading me to metaphor, and a poem
in which I navigated gratitude
to him and — turning, turning — grief for her.

2. *North Broadway & Grand*

— for Owen, the Dancing Policeman of St. Louis

O, when she died
he was the traffic cop
again, the ballet dancer
so gracefully

threading a city
through his hands,
only this time he was there
at the crossroads

to lead her home,
his sister, through
the deepening dark,
no light but that

of his presence,
his only uniform
the look he gave her
as every move he made

the whole rushing hour long
signalled he was
close enough to her
to die himself.

"The most difficult corner
in the city. The most
expensive equipment
couldn't manage it."

Put Dacey in. And the human
touch eased
the knot, jam, block,
and everyone got home

safe, everyone.

ESKIMO JOE

How can I not remember I
rubbed noses with my father in
his lonely bed when I was ten?
Forty years ago. He's ninety

as he's telling me this as if
it happened yesterday. "Before
we'd fall asleep. You stayed over
Fridays. It always made you laugh."

I don't forget the little room
he lived in for a year or so
after the divorce. Just two
of us were a crowd. Leave your dream

outside. Was there even a chair?
And the rented bed was so small
he'd press himself against the wall
to give me space to sleep. To hear

of such touching touches me — here
at the heartbreak tip of my nose.
"*You* know," he says, "like Eskimos."
I see an ice floe and many long years

as someone tries to live on it.
When Joe married Rose, whose perfume
meant spring had opened up his room,
he rubbed his nose deep in her wet

promise, though in this late, dry autumn
he would stir my memory. What

I think of is a book about
beavers I once read and the time

that sociable tribe spent a whole
far northern winter in their tight
domed quarters the wind rushed to bite
through, passing the days in gentle

grooming, low sounds, bodily touch.
The author was fortunate to observe
a particular "expressive
behavior pattern": at approach,

one creature nuzzled the other's face.
The air was cold. "Do you remember?"
Now I smell the frozen river.
"Oh, yes," I tell him. "I do. Yes."

READING WHILE DRIVING

I drive and dive
for a few words,
then surface to the road,
holding them in my ear,
until I see all is clear

and dive again.
I'm a danger
to myself,
other cars,
the piecemealed poem,

though maybe like any modern
I love fragments:
this phrase, all that was left
on the stone after the crash
of a civilization. Read into it

everything, a history
of someone at the helm
who wasn't there,
who was dreaming,
and repeat the ritual

of its few syllables
as the best way to face
your futures, the one
oncoming, the other
crowding fast from behind.

FOR THE GOD POSEIDON

*"Each Trident II submarine will carry the
destructive power equivalent to 7,200
Hiroshimas."*
— *Greenpeace Monthly*

Full fathom five thy trident lay
for years, where you, apparently
in some great hurry to get away,
dropped it, your only weaponry.

Most likely you fled unbelief,
to live disguised elsewhere, but with
you gone the sea became unsafe,
the cruising grounds for other faiths.

And one such faith outswam the rest,
swallowing whole schools, and flashing
razor-fins. It was the biggest
and the best, and sent waves crashing.

It exuded one power above all,
the intimate metamorphosis,
in darkened caves working its will,
atom by atom, wet kiss by wet kiss.

You would not know your spear now, which
(help us) has suffered a sea-change
into something more strange than rich,
though it cost treasures to rearrange.

This missilehead that was a prong —
no sea-nymph strokes it with her hand,
idling in sea-love the day long.
This guidance system was our mind.

Ding-dong. Full fathom five, past reefs
the monster slides. Impossible,
we say, who are between beliefs,
between the knellings of a bell.

THE NEIGHBORS

*"Ask yourself who you would prefer as a
neighbor — Saddam Hussein or George Bush."*
— Mary Jane Laub, *Christian Science
Monitor,* Feb. 25, 1991

I walk out my front door
to enjoy the summer evening,
the silk hand of a breeze.
Immediately eastward,
Saddam is watering his lawn.
He sees me and waves absentmindedly,
absorbed in the sound of the drops slapping grass.
On the west side, George reclines
in a lounge chair, a newspaper folded on his lap
as he looks at nothing in particular,
a car passing, a bird hopping at a distance.

They're good neighbors.
It's true I worried when they moved in,
one right after the other.
I had heard stories.
And there I was between them.
But I have seen them pass each other on the street
with an acknowledging nod
and even sometimes chat for a while
before they part with smiles and touches
on the arm, the back.
From time to time I borrow things, too,
a ladder from Saddam, a drill from George.
As I said, they're good neighbors.

Only occasionally
a small hand pushes up

from the ground their lots enclose,
breaking the level green,
the fingers uncurling
toward the light
and moving with an appearance
of great expressiveness,
and then only briefly
before a small engine starts up
and low blades
whirr quietly, restoring
the uninterrupted
and peaceful expanse
of the neighborhood
we take such pride and pleasure in
on summer evenings
like this one.

THE NEW AMERICAN STATIONS OF THE CROSS

1.
Pilate condemns Jesus
to watch twelve straight
hours of television,
consume two six-packs of beer,
three bags of chips, and four
hot dogs on white Wonder buns.

2.
Jesus' side is pierced
by the dull rhetoric
of presidential candidates,
who drink his blood.

3.
Jesus falls the first time,
under the federal budget deficit.

4.
Veronica wipes the face
of Jesus with a handy, pre-dampened,
perfumed towelette
that stings his wounds.

5.
Jesus falls the second time,
under the burden of
National Security
and the New World Order.

6.
Japan offers to carry
Jesus' cross
at a very attractive interest rate.

7.
Jesus meets his mother,
who introduces him
to several members
of her lesbian support group.

8.
The infrastructure
along the Via Dolorosa
having gone to hell,
Jesus falls the third time
but is rescued
by a political action committee
interested in
His Father's vote.

9.
Jesus, who carries no cash
in his small loin cloth,
is stripped of his credit cards,
which have no limits.

10.
Jesus is nailed to a cross
of wood from an old-growth forest.

11.
Jesse Helms,
wrapped in stars and stripes
against the cold Golgotha wind,
watches all night

to make sure no one
digs up the cross
and sticks it in a jar of piss.

12.
Jesus is taken down
from the cross
because 64% of the people
surveyed in a Gallup poll
approve of such action
while only 32% disapprove
and 4% don't know what they think.

13.
Jesus is laid
in a tomb
converted from
a defunct
Savings and Loan
vault.

14.
The Supreme Court rules
God is guilty
of reverse discrimination
in letting only a Jew
rise from the dead.

FOUR MEN IN A CAR

"The ugliest thing in the world is the sight of
four men in a car."
> — David Bailey, photographer, quoted in
> *American Photographer,* Sept.1988

We sit in the womanless car,
maleness twice-squared, going nowhere.

Two in front and two in back,
in the Jill-less car, Jack, Jack, Jack, and Jack.

We know how ugly we are,
but what can we do? We live here.

The truth is none of us can drive,
though our horsepower is impressive.

It may be a meeting's our goal,
or a game, or something illegal,

but it's all the same. The deadest end.
So we tell jokes. You know the kind.

Outside the car the women walk
and run and leap or make such talk

as prompts their hands to fly about
in ways ours, cramped inside, cannot.

Close, but not too, we don't move much;
it's accidental when we touch.

Oh, there's nothing as ugly as we,
four men in a car, not five or three.

To breathe, we roll our windows down,
and then we roll them up again.

MYSTERY FOOTBALL

Someone no one has seen,
not even the players,
sends in plays from the sidelines.

What seem to be fumbles
are acts of love,
exchanges
between what seem to be enemies.
And all interceptions
form a triangle
of sender, intended,
and receiver.
Play over, the triangles remain.
They collect,
up and down the field,
like ghosts.

In each pileup, a player confesses
a lifetime secret.
In each huddle, everything
is denied.

A runner twists and turns,
he is unwinding
a signature.
It is not his,
he only knows
he twists, turns, and,
after a beautiful though ambiguous gain,
goes down.

At halftime, there is a death.
But it does not count.
The clock is not running.

When play resumes, a long pass
arcs with an achingly poignant
curve.
Everyone catches it.

The game ends suddenly, with the hidden ball trick.
No one can find it.
The quarterback forgets where he hid it.
The players look for it
until the sun
is tackled from behind.
Then they go home,
the score knotted
around their hearts.

That night, out of those hearts rises a dream
of the ball sailing through the uprights.
It keeps rising,
past the outstretched hands of fans,
over the scoreboard,
and never comes down:
it is one long continuous
extra point.

COUPON LOVE

Where are the dotted lines
the bargain
in this bed?
I am lost
among the all too human
flesh
that won't total up
in pennies.
One kiss
or thrust saved
is not one earned.
Benjamin,
the soul
that is to say
the body
is never
on weekly special
though I have waited
and waited.
I want to cut
along the breasts
the penis
find the right angles
I call home
but the curves
come and come
natives
over the hill
waves
of an endless circle.
Clip, clip

the sound
is a mere memory
the numbers
dance along the edge of the scissors
only to mock
showing their genitals
their obscene
abstractions
aglitter
with desire.

THE DEATHBED PLAYBOY

My old man, dying, motioned I should lean
down close to him to catch his whispered wish:
"I want to see a Playboy magazine."
It was enough to make a grown son blush.
He was ninety-one. Retired from farming.
Iowa Republican and Catholic.
Was Hugh Hefner's monthly Princess Charming
to be his final angel? Did Death trick
old men into confusing one striptease
with another: a bare breast with a soul
peeled out of its flesh? But I aimed to please.
He had the right to make himself a fool.

The family had gone home to eat. Perhaps
his waiting until now to tell me meant
this was to be our secret. Just two chaps
having a little fun. Father-son in-
timacy. Two on one. What a way to go!
The drugstore downstairs had a stack. Could this
have been standard procedure? Boost the flow
of adrenaline with skin. Better a kiss,
imagined or not, than more pills and shots.
I bought. I didn't tell the pretty girl
behind the counter my dad had the hots
for Miss June, or that Death wanted to curl
up with him. I just wished her a nice night
and went back to his room, bearing the mag
toward him like a priest with a last rite,
except I was thinking of Hef in drag
as Florence Nightingale. I hid my grin,
as if it would have made a difference:
Pop was in and out of consciousness; even
awake, he seemed only flirting with sense.

Because his hands worked badly, like his tongue,
I helped him find the centerfold. Miss June,
red-haired and gifted, had at least one thing
in common with him: she was lying down.
And by a window, too, but old-gold light
streamed through hers in rapt attendance on her;
through his, half-light cowered to think of night
and all but ignored him; and while the flowers
by her left hip couldn't take their day's eyes
off her scandalous breasts, his bouquet was mum
about his chances and only exhaled sighs
of oxygen, limply. Tubes made him hum,
but her look clearly said, No strings attached.
Miss June was pure socialized medicine.

I couldn't read his face well as I watched
him take her in. His eyes traversed her skin
like manned snowshoes across a wintry plain,
awkward, slow, chilled. But he made the journey.
The while he did we didn't speak. My brain
was travelling at the speed of light, gone horny
with awe — at his strange request — and questions —
why, and why, and why. Maybe even he
didn't know. Bare truth lay behind bastions
of sheer cloth. Step up closer, Boys, and see.
Was this a farewell to Woman, her heft,
hearty, handsome, what once he hied to, wived?
Or the microbody of the earth itself,
home, rolling-hilled, deep-valleyed? Or the curved
universe laid dreamily out across vast space
like Mom at nursing time, milky, brimfull?
Or none of these, but simply the last trace
of an old girlfriend, never forgotten. Or all.

A nurse poked her head in. Everything okay?
I leaned to shield the folly. (Father's? Son's?)

Just fine, thanks. Just a little deathbed play,
I didn't add. If she noticed our men's
club meeting in progress, she gave no sign,
a pro through and through, but only a dry smile,
then vanished, leaving us once more alone
with a simpler woman, two-dimensional,
whom I was still trying to complicate.
(The old boy had one long last leg to travel.)
She didn't ask for it, that someone make her
up — woman's body as another clean slate
for improving — but mentally I chalked, Acre:
if he could plow one more, he wouldn't die,
a lifetime's practice argued. Better Red —
(real name, Sue King) whose spread was obviously
a June field (jeune fille!) craving seed — than dead.
And then I saw the trick. Hers. She was It,
Death, the very thing, disguised as supple
and willing flesh, bedroom joy, youth, to flat-
ter him: We'd make such a lovely couple.
I shuddered: not only at the subterfuge
(imagined) but also at the sudden thought I
was a deathbed playboy, too; my younger age
meant nothing. I could see it in her eye:
Soon, she said. Soon I'll tire of him for you.
I knew her word was good. The Honest Woman.

Slowly he pushed her away, as if all through,
and looked up at me, a sound half low moan
and half speech on his lips. What did you say?
He tried again but swallowed every word.
Was that "thanks," "shanks," or "winks"? "hard," "bared,"
    or "bird"?
Then, just as I shrugged at him, who looked so alone
struggling to talk, a wave of pure dismay
engulfed me: what if I had earlier misheard?

What if his request to view a playmate
was intended to get himself a bed pan? a fluffed
pillow? water? or his lost words did not
ask but gave: were a first: told how much he loved
his only son? And I had burdened him
with my madness? If so, he must have been no less
amazed than I at our trio like a dream.
And one of his last acts was therefore a kindness,
to humor me. Who was taking care of whom?
I wanted to cry and laugh and disappear
all at once. What I did, no doubt, was look dumb.
But he let nothing show — being either sheer
grace or just weak — except a sleepiness
he gave in to, or feigned, for my poor sake.
I was off the hook. I wanted to kiss
him, and so did, on the forehead, that quick
sanctuary of a dying man's last thoughts.
And better: imagined Red's ghost leaned out
of her picture to kiss him, too. Her spirit-
breasts swung like tower bells to celebrate
a life, and I liked her for her tender show
but shut the pages on her anyway
and bagged her, because I heard the family
coming back. They found me smoothing a sheet. How
is he? an uncle asked, and I said, Fair,
thinking of fair maidens and fair-haired boys.
Asleep — now, truly — he looked all innocence there
and ready for the sacrifice. No choice.
When someone suggested I take a break,
I went, smuggling Red out like contraband,
and headed for a bar. Scotch on the rocks,

which I lifted in salute to last stands
everywhere, and companions for that time.
The bartender joined in, who got paid to agree.
I bought the house drinks (a small crowd), no rhyme
or reason, just fool generosity.

THE WHEEL

You came back to me
with a kiss.
And then I sat beside you
as you brushed your hair.
We talked about
things being all right again.
It was so good
I said this must be a dream.
You said, No, it's real.
And I could tell it was.

But, of course, it wasn't.

I awoke from a rare
afternoon nap
beside our Fay, still curled
into an eight-year-old's
sound sleep, and her dog —
three creatures full of need
on a big bed.
      And when I heard
the hamster in the next room,
I knew that the rough
music of your brush
pulling through your hair
was actually the rasping
of him on his wheel
as he drove it round
and round the way someone
in search of an answer

might drive his own brain
upon itself until
he goes crazy
finding nothing
over and over again
at a terrifically high speed.

II

WALT WHITMAN'S SUNDAY WITH
THE INSANE

It was in Canada, Ontario,
 while visiting his doctor friend
that Whitman on a Sunday came to know
 the beauty in a broken mind.

It was at Dr. Bucke's establishment
 for the mad, confused, and weird
that Whitman followed where three hundred went
 to sit in pews before the Lord.

He thought the asylum a model of its sort
 for his much-loved cleanliness and cheer,
and gladly that morning as honored guest sat
 by the hall's pulpit, in an armchair.

Better yet, his chair angled in such a way
 he saw the faces of the crowd,
and as the sermon's words held lofty sway,
 he studied what those faces showed.

Many were old, and quaintly bonneted —
 his mother dead now seven years! —
and not one horrific; all looked instead
 like faces framed in old pictures.

A light through the windows on one side
 touched the sick array with health,
and whitewashed floorboards shone as if to hide
 the losses of an early wealth.

But not completely hide. He looked behind
 the minister's "peace of God

that passeth what a man can understand,"
and saw the shipwrecks in the blood.

For up in the air, but pressing near,
  the slumped body of Jesus Christ
told of throes, and a swamped, final hour,
  where Whitman pondered in the midst,

pondered mysteries, storms of love, wrong, and greed
  that drove some willy-nilly here
to live, and not — spent casualties of need,
  each soul its own civil war.

And then, beneath the exemplary wounds,
  he suffered a vision of sacrifice:
this motley, these poor creatures of the winds —
  they'd all gone crazy in his place.

(The chair groaned as the poet shifted his weight
  as in a gust. But the idea blew
harder, like some unholy ghost not yet
  done with what it had to do.)

And brother Eddy, too. A lightning rod
  of lunacy, as it were. He took
the shot from God that Walt's head could be good.
  Now Walt sat back. And his hands shook.

As if to save him then, the choir began —
  Lead, Kindly Light, lead Thou me on —
above the sounds of a melodeon,
  and soon a few inmates joined in.

Whitman loved, of course, his opera.
  Parlor gestures were not for him.
But never had an aria appassionata
  pierced him like Fr. Newman's hymn.

And old man Whitman sat in his armchair
 and made his "eye-sweeps," as he said,
and saw out as if into a crazed mirror,
 and sang as loud as he could.

HARRY STAFFORD: WHITMAN AT TIMBER CREEK

My parents told me I should treat him well;
he was a famous poet, taken ill.
He seemed less famous to me than simply lame,
old, near-broken, a man who came to our farm
three summers in a row to convalesce.
This was after the Civil War. I guess
the years he spent beside the beds of sick
and dying soldiers had their price — the stick
he leaned on heavily getting to the creek.
That creek, which ran below our house, was like
his bed — he'd lie in it — the air and sun
a nurse and doctor making daily rounds.
With Nature as his veterans' hospital —
though unenlisted, he earned the name, for all
he did, or else the word means narrowly —
he took his medicine from any tree.

Actually, he wrestled saplings, but that
came later; at first, he just wanted to sit.
He had a chair I'd move from spot to spot,
depending on the way the sunlight hit.
He'd sit for hours, basking like an old toad,
unless he wrote in one of the little homemade
books he always carried. I remember
their edges curled, like dropped leaves. I'd swear
they even came brand-new from his pocket that way.
Oftentimes he'd ask me to identify
a certain tree or flower he didn't know,
and if I did, he'd jot the name down. So
I learned the names to better answer him.
It took me years to see his friendly game.

He flattered me, since he most likely knew
most names, and spurred my interest in what grew.

The bees were medicine, too. He loved to walk
among them in the lane they loved to flock
to in clouds, chains of clouds, a whole system,
as it were, of bee-weather that took him in
until he'd disappear in one great hum,
including his own. He called it vocalism,
whether he vied with bees or not, pure sound
not song nor words but what the underground
would attempt of music, if it had the will.
I'd hear the roarings of an animal
and know it was only the poet by the creek,
pretending, for his health, he couldn't speak.

Then I saw him roll naked in the mud
and thought he *was* an animal, or mad.
In the dell we had a marlpit through which
a streamlet ran, creating an ooze such
as God must have fashioned on the first day.
My father used it to fertilize the rye.
That first summer even, Whitman's habit
of sunbathing creekside in his birthday suit
had begun, and I, until the paralysis
relented some, helped him undress and dress.
He called me Nurse Harry, and said my kind
ways to him must somehow someday come round
home to me, because everything came round.
The next year, he felt strong enough to roam
at will, and when he found the hole with loam
as thick as paste, and black, and up to his knee,
he declared muck's medicinal quality
and waded in. That summer I got rich
charging friends of mine a penny each
to watch the primal creature in the dell

perform his strange antics. I charged the girls
double. We could see him, but not he us.
He always thought he was alone — unless
he knew, and didn't want to spoil our fun,
or thought we could learn something from an old man.
We did: how to smear ourselves all over
with mud, then let the spring's little rivers
wash it away as we lay on our backs.
And rub our skin with leaves and twigs to make
it glow with ruddiness, then soothe the raw
places with creamy mud, and water's flow.
Or walk mud-flecked along the banks, as if
just made, and like God, but a little stiff.
Except Adam didn't wear a straw hat
as Whitman always did, nor, surely, recite
swatches of Shakespeare in operatic tones
while watching slime squish up between his toes.
If parents later asked us where we were,
we'd mumble something about literature.

He only half-recovered. Even Nature
could not undo the damage of the war.
He liked to say the boys did him more good
than he did them; I'd say they gave his need
to give himself away an opening.
Still, that third summer with us he was strong
enough to practice what he called "health-pulls."
He'd yank and tug for hours on young trees, curl
them down then let them lift him up — oak, beech,
holly. He told me stories of the speech
of trees, dryads and hamadryads, how
a certain sapling he hugged just might know
who the visitor was and that it passed
its virtue on to him through his caress.
I almost believed him then; I almost believe
him now. I certainly believe his love

for trees. One long rainy day he sat under
a pine, body against bark, all surrender.
Then he was gone. I like to think he took
back with him to Camden part of our creek
to draw on during his last years. Water ran
through his room then, and the bees came at the end.
Oddly, as I've aged, he's gotten less crazy.
I'm going out now to wrestle a tree.

THE BURIAL

"Burial of Little Walter Whitman"
— Headline in *Philadelphia Ledger,*
July 20, 1876

He died of heat, like summer's toy,
Walt Whitman's nephew, perfect joy.

The coffin that they laid him in
was white and matched his infant skin,

this only child's — a sibling would
have eased the fact that he was dead

for father George and mother Lou,
though neighbor children came to strew

the babe with fresh geranium leaves
and tuberoses on his sleeves.

Beside the coffin, in a chair
as great as all his great white hair,

the poet sat, but not alone,
for children claimed him as their own —

a boy encircled by each arm;
a girl between, whose golden storm

of ringlets spilled into his lap,
whence to his face she looked straight up

as if to make an inquiry
concerning him who lay nearby.

And old Walt said, the story goes,
"I see you don't know what it is,"

giving a nod toward Master Death,
"Well, I don't either, that's the truth,"

and drew the three together so
their faces sank in his beard's snow.

WALT WHITMAN FALLS ASLEEP OVER FLORENCE NIGHTINGALE'S *NOTES ON NURSING*

The rat clings swaying to the tentpole near
the sleeping soldier's head. Fiery eyes shine;
it is the snout of war, death's tickling whiskers,
and a tail that sweeps all young men into line.
I'm paralyzed; my hands grip my white suit
until like lightning from the west a bright
blow, shaft of steel, catches the hatching skull
square, and the black bulk plumbs past with a splat.
Hail Deadeye Florence with her parasol!
She raises to her lips the silver tip
and blows, as if it smoked, hot from the kill.
"Time for our rounds," she says, whose dark curls peep
out from beneath the lacy cap that frames
the face that launched a dozen suitors' dreams,
though all sank like freighters in the Bosporus.
So where am I? Virginia? The Crimea?
With miserably bit Brits? Missourians? This place
swarming with shadows, where walls flap, could be a
purgatorial hospital at any front
perched on the jerry-built hot roof of hell.
But eyes here follow one flame they pray won't
go out, that's tall in the lamp of Nightingale.
She carries it aloft from bed to bed,
handing the icon to me each time she halts
to bend, touch, talk. Then I admire the shrunk head
of an English general slung from her belt,
trophy of her war with her War Office. Oh,
this lady has teeth herself, to tear the heart
from Army rules that prop the official show
but help no wounded jumbled in a cart.
And that's why, look, wherever her silhouette

ripples across a pillow as we move,
lips curse-heavy press with a touch as light
as a girl's against coarse cloth, imprinting a love
I do not envy, having known it, too.
Thus, tandem dray horses, we work this ward
that is our home — our home because it's here
the needs of others tell us what to do —
she the tender commander, I the bearded
mother, she dressed like night, I all cheer.
Call us nursing's perfect, if strangest, pair.
Now we pass outdoors between tents, each star
a signalling patient transformed by our care,
to meet directly in our path a great heap
of what, under an oak, campfire-lit, seems
merely a disarray of cordwood but up
close turns into tossed amputated limbs.
I hear my voice, thin, wind among the flames.
"Once the merest boy said to me, 'Go fetch
my arm back, would you, please, Sir, for I forgot
to keep my gold wedding band and will catch
grief from Mary if I come home without it.'"
Light dances, leggy, atop the danceless legs,
pours liquid armor like a skin on skin.
Now her voice, grim, writhes to undo some knot.
"Their leaders called them brutes, treated them like dogs.
I stood beside each when the knife went in
and know: the lower the rank, the braver the man.
Death at Scutari? Seldom by Russian gun.
My statistics made Whitehall see what's worse —
filth. We discovered, late, our water ran
straight through the carcass of a long-dead horse."
We stand like tourists at a monument,
the guide books shut, inadequate, the thing
before us wholly other while also of course
our very own, what we would deny, but can't.
The moon's implausibly cool on its string.

When next my partner turns her face to me,
she's suddenly aged, or like an actress, young,
made up so: lines pencilled in, hair powdery.
I am her audience, to whom she would confess:
"My poor men endured so much. They spilled blood,
I only ink. There were so many, and I've been bad
to have left them in their graves. I did not kiss
enough. Jowett keeps telling me I must try
to think of all I did. But I cannot.
If only I might improve my history
bedside, because you've dreamed me here tonight . . ."
Dreamed? I feel the bruising ground underfoot,
hear the bright clink of gear, see the night sky,
and tell her this is real. "Then they can die,"
and her words make little flares at her lips
before she spins away and her lamp swings up
to orbit, devotee, its central body but
is thrust off course into the dark where it
finds, among a world of tents, one small tent
we enter, bowing through the low door as if
to him, the lone occupant, whom we know —
impossibly, he is the same who lost his life
at both Manassas and Sebastopol,
alive again, for us. His long yellow
hair's pillowed rings snare our thoughts, and he is pale.
We find stools and sit together beside
the cot lest he ever has to turn his head.
Then she, who loves to avoid "And how are you?"
starts with, "Point to where it hurts most," and he,
seeing us seeing him suffer, points to her, to me.
Light gutters where solicitousness blew.
"Is there anything you'd like us to do?"
He's thinking. Then smiles. He knows something. "Sing."
Sing? Glances pass between us visitors.
"A grand piece, please. From the stage. This tent's poor."
Opera was my heaven when I was young.

With luck, my heaven will be an opera box,
from overture to delicious tragic climax.
But Nightingale? "Do you know opera?"
She's asking *me*. ". . . a girlhood weakness of mine
insufficiently indulged." I chance, "*Norma?*
'Casta Diva'?" Chaste goddess. To the moon.
Her eyes widen as if I'd read her mind
and she begins Bellini's aria my own
goddess, Marietta Alboni, stormed New York
with in '52, asking the unveiled face
spargi in terra — to bathe the earth in peace.
All camp sounds stop as if the woods cried hark.
Alboni's back, played by this Nightingale,
who elbows me to do my part, and I,
sitting up straight, assume the attendants' roles —
we fear Rome and second our mistress's will.
Thus Whitman and Nightingale, low and high,
sing better than by rights we should,
as in a dream, and our too sick friend, mid-
aria, applauds, perforce weakly, and nods his head.
I see in a flash the Times' WALT AND FLORENCE
STUN BROOKLYN — this is *Brooklyn?* — WITH THEIR SONG
and can already taste the praise, though once
the fancies pass, I know something is wrong.
I know we are not singing just for fun.
The small space suddenly has filled with ghosts,
pressing ghosts who are all ears, every one.
Critics? Lost souls alert for any mistake,
an off-key note, the rhythm even the slightest
bit awry. Our charge depends on our music:
if one of us goes flat, he dies. I look
at her — she's beautiful — her open mouth —
at him she'll live for her remaining years,
and think of all rats twitching everywhere,
then summon up this singing nurse's faith.

III

GOD CONSIDERS THE OPTIONS
FOR HUMAN PROCREATION

It will not be with thoughts,
for their thoughts will run thin,
will not even reach to their ankles.

Nor with their hands,
for they will fumble:
doors will stay locked,
pens will drop,
rings will roll away.

The legs? No.
They shall always be
running away.

The mouth. That is a hole
to be filled.
But they should be able to say
"Love" as they make my image.
It shall not be the mouth.

The eyes. The eyes widening
with amazement until
men and women
step out of them.
But these will be easily blinded.
These will shut fearfully
before the brightest lights.

Nor the nose and ears.
Collectors of small objects,
these will be too busy.

Therefore with their loins,
where the body forks.
At these crossroads
let them spend
their lives. Whatever comes
and goes here day
after day will give them
their news of the world.

TERESA

*1. She Writes Offering to Buy for Her Son, in
   Minnesota, an Electric Blanket*

I may be eightysome years old but I know
no woman in her right mind wants to screw
in a house whose temperature is kept so low
the cats sneeze all day and her hands turn blue.
What you and Suzie Q. do with yourselves
under covers a foot deep — trust me — only passes
for love: it's premature burial. Or else
you toss the damned things off and freeze your asses.
So for her sake if not yours, let me buy you
a good electric blanket for your igloo.
I didn't raise an idiot, don't act like one.
I deserve a completely defrosted son.
And heat soothes old bones better than a pill.
You don't have such things, Mr. Young? You will.

2. Crepuscule for Mother

The old woman's world shrinks
to what she eats, bowel movements.
And the world shrinks with her, in sympathy.

Why not go out from earth miles
and miles with the expanding aether
the older we get and leave a trail
of floating breadcrumbs so the others
can find us if they dare?

She is imploding like a black star,
my mother,
and I fear her rim,
her whirlpool self.

To thin like beaten gold, that's the way,
a film on being,
not collect in a hard mass
and drop through the center.

Cloud-exit, taking various shapes,
animals, maps of exotic countries,
abstract cine-vapors.

Mother, the night sky calls.
Open your wings.
Tour the stars.
I will cling
to your hem,
as always.

I do not want you to be a small
hard rock burning in my hand.

In deep space,
a cool wind
is a river
to set ourselves upon,
trailing fingers
like vain questions
in our wake,
that groove the black water
though we have let them go.

WHY JESUS WAS CRUCIFIED

I thought they were Georgia O'Keefe's flowers, or
struggling pencil imitations of them,
but then I saw the mirror under the bed,
where I'd found the artist's pad, and knew my wife
had been drawing herself between the legs.
Soon-to-be-ex-, that is. I was moving out,
divorce a certainty, but not before
she'd started pursuing what her therapist,
I came to learn, had recommended, this
study, a way to begin anew, I guess,
sight, insight, a long overdue and deep-
rinsed apprehension of her central self.
I imagined her on her back, head sharply
propped by pillows, nightgown pulled belly-high
out of the way, knees flexed as in birthing,
one hand holding the long-handled mirror
flashing between her legs as she tipped it —
I think now of a dentist maneuvering
to get right the angle of his own in a
mouth, and vagina dentata — the other
against the pad that lay flat on the bed,
eyes concentrating as they wove between
the image and the moving point of lead.
Imagining all that, the awkwardness,
I thought how lucky we are, men, the obvious
ones, ours always in plain view, with not the
slightest intention of hiding away.
You want to see it? There it is. So what's new?
But there she lay, working at acquiring
a vision we take for granted. Is that
what husbands are for, to act as reflectors
for wives' self-knowledge? And our marriage failed
because I was only a cracked, dim mirror?

The perfect world a perfectly polished
surface. I slid the equipment back to where
I'd found it and kept packing, wondering
as I did what dear dead Grandma McGinn
would say. Irish immigrant, she never
missed a daily rosary. And bore nine kids,
a religious duty, no questions asked.
I knew what: "Jesus, Mary, and Joseph," as
she made the sign of the cross, "what in the
good name of God is this world coming to?"
But only one of those three invoked might know,
who found the feathers of the holy ghost
between her legs soft but a dull mirror.
But maybe Jesus, too. Maybe Jesus
held the mirror there for Mary Magdalene
as she drew, knowing he had the angle right
by her smile. And maybe that's why the Romans
killed Jesus, for assisting at one of
those births, where a woman emerges out
of herself, onto a glass, onto paper,
with nothing renderable to Caesar.

PORTRAIT, WITH LIGHTNING ROD

My daughter hates the sun and loves the rain.
She likes it overcast, a touch of pain

on everything. The leaves have such a gloss
when wet, it makes a shining of our loss.

She's drawn to coastal fog or low-slung clouds
that bring the sky down to its knees, and shrouds

the wind blows in to drape across the day
comfort her, promising the dark will stay.

Seattle, London, Ireland's west coast — these
are magic places guaranteed to please

because the air is silk enough to wear.
She dreams of growing up and moving there.

I don't know when it was inclemency
first touched her so: the night she came to be,

most likely: I drove her mother through a storm
of snow, and birth made falling skies the norm.

In fact, we'd thought of making "Storm" her name,
but then she slept, and made the storm go tame.

She wishes now we'd named her so. I think
she'd like it as a bridge across the brink

between the outside and inside worlds she knows
are facing mirrors. At least, each year she grows

more natural to me: she moves like air
when change is coming in, her plunging hair

a cataract beneath which lovers stand,
her eyes a center quickening the land.

MACAROONS

I brought four dozen macaroons to school
because Nora in *A Doll's House* loved them so.
How sweet each bite she took against the rule!

Her husband thought she was a child, the fool,
and wouldn't let her eat her fill. His no
was law. She taught him lessons in her school.

But first she had to eat his ridicule
and swallow thoughts she didn't dare let show
(how sweet those dark stirrings against the rule!).

The students gobbled up the teaching tool,
quick learners all, and wanted more, although
I'd brought dozens of macaroons to school.

Each had a dab of jelly like a jewel.
One crumb told everything there was to know
about sweetness won from a life of rule.

That whole class passed the test — like Nora, who'll
always give the right answer, *Freedom, hello,*
as, armed with macaroons, she exits to school
in the sweet world where possibilities rule.

SHACKING UP

We built a shack around us
and shacked and shacked
the whole shack long.

Up was only one way,
there were down, and right, and left,
and a way without a name

Jesus took when he went four ways
on the cross at once to make his father smile
and say that was good.

There were no doors or windows,
we saw to that, we built that shack
out of impenetrable sighs and whispers.

Shack me, shack me again
were the words that couldn't escape
except from our lips.

We didn't palace up, or condo up,
or tent, nomadically or outsydoorsy, up,
but only shack, what's falling down,

no status but ourselves in it,
something out back the sleek
world on wheels getting somewhere

has no time for,
warped, a wonder, by nature,
nor made to last, collapsing

over only eons like a star to a black
hole, two stars happy to make
a nighttime spectacle of themselves,

a skyful forming the constellation Shack.

STUDY

— for the painter Edward Evans

A man before a painting is tempted
to see a bed. Beds are tempting,
as paintings are. Some lines suggest
a satin sheet pulled taut, and who
but lovers sleep on satin sheets?
The man is pleased to see the sheet,
the bed, the lovers outside the frame,

although a rosy color at an edge,
some spreading harvest flame, a mild
rebuke to icy sheets, is clear
enough, a sign there is no sheet,
no bed, no lover with his loved,
only a surface spread with paint,
where some artist lies to dream
as if upon a sheet upon a bed,
and leaves a sign he lies because
he would be honest, like a lover.
The man before the painting knows this.

Knows it, and, no matter, sees
what he would see, what he is tempted
to see. As when later, walking home,
tempted to see a world of sense,
an order framing everything,
love in the eyes of two who pass,
and the smeared sky a painting, illusion
he walks under, happily,
himself perhaps another brushstroke,
intentional or not, that adds
meaning to the composition,

he sees it. All. Tempted, in weakness,
he gives in, in strength. Or so

he is tempted to think as, suddenly tired,
he lies in bed that night, tracing
with his finger like a brush the lines
of a taut sheet, of his lover's arm,
of his own thought with the brushstroke
of his words, and seeing again
the painting he had stood before
and entered, in and out at once.
Its rosy edge is spreading for him
now approaching sleep, like some dream
about to overtake another dream.

TRIO

1. The Musician

"Bach is always making the sacred
secular and the secular sacred."
— Bill McGlaughlin, Minnesota Public Radio

In the great nave of the church,
we eat noodles and throw dice,
while at lunch in the cafe
a man sinks to his knees,
muttering prayers
and touching the floor with his head.

A minister delivers a sermon
that sounds suspiciously like a recipe
for *coq au vin*,
while someone else has hung
beautiful laundry out to dry
on the wide-open arms of a cross.

We're confused
but happy to be so,
unclear as to whether
that was God who just walked by
or a musician
on her way to a concert,
the whole next world
squeezed into her black case.

2. *Bachspeed*

The start of Bach's Toccata and Fugue in D
Minor on my car's tape deck drives down my
foot like the organist's onto the pedal
only now gas surges and my right arm
waves me homeward until unbeknownst to
musically souped-up me I'm ten miles an
hour over the limit and attracting
flashing red lights into my slipstream like
arpeggios though I'm still humming the Master
as I pull over park and jive my way
back to the squad car to face some other
music explaining as I get in how
it was Bach's fault, Officer, Bach's, and he
says he doesn't see anybody else in
my car and starts writing out a ticket
forty bucks worth the price of a good seat
at a rock concert Johann Sebastian
und his Rollenden Steine Bach meaning
brook jawohl and therefore he who tumbles
little stones as the music descends from
heaven to us but it's too late to slow down
so I resume humming fingering the dash
confident music's not illegal just
stopping it before it's over is which
is why I left the tape playing and even
turned up the volume as I slid out of
my church pew on wheels and stepped back here where now
Patrolman Jensen's pen scratches a near
perfect counterpoint to E. Power Biggs' hands
chasing themselves up and down the keyboard
like cars in some cops-and-killers movie's
last frames and I want to tell my cop fugue
you merely as a joke of course but doubt the
depth of his musical appreciation

and anyway he's giving me edgy looks
as I start practicing my Baroque scat
like some jazz singer in a time warp and
later stays behind me in close harmony
for a mile or two after my release
as air escapes from great brass pipes but I
don't mind for Sheep May Safely Graze has rolled
into play and I'm going slow enough now
to test his patience and let myself smile
at the thought that while music follows laws
I know a law that follows music until
I turn off on a dirt road guaranteed
to lay a thick coat of dust on my angel's
shiny steel shell and he demurs choosing
the clean whine of asphalt and making me
feel like Bach on Sundays in the choir loft
improvising himself out of trouble.

3. Musica

I remember how in Spain
when the bullfight lagged —
the bull stubborn and still,
the matador at a loss, waving his arms —
the spectators, become impatient,
would chant, *Musica, musica!*
and beg from the band
of musicians in the stands
vivid strains to put a rhythm
under the ritual's participants
and get them moving.

Now, moved to the country
amidst the rolling returns
of the seasons,
I frequently cry, *Musica!*
and set spinning what moves me
through the house, into
and out of chores, or transports me
outside even, to bend in the garden,
as a bird and a violin
discover each other
in my ear, while, at other times,
the phonograph silent, my pen in hand,
I would have a poem, its music,
its particular rhythms
and strongest measures,
equally move me.

No doubt on my deathbed,
as the light takes hours
and hours to fail
completely,
I will call,

Musica, musica!
wanting as always
something to happen,
anything,
to carry me away.

ROMANCE

1.
Those little flames
as you prepare
your dinner for one.

2.
The shadows
look at you
from across the room.

3.
All the strangers
inside you
come forward,
letters of introduction
perfuming their hands.

4.
A little silence — that moment at lunch today — is
absence, but this great silence, that has moved in from
the stars, and down across the hills, through the trees
and into this room, is touch.

5.
The long-stemmed rose
of breath,
a bouquet
dispersed
in the gathering.

6.
Do you take this woman
whose scarlet gown
trails into your blood?

I do.

SOL O SOMBRA

"Sol o sombra?"
the ticketseller at the bullfight would ask,
and week after week I'd reply, "Sombra,"
paying the extra pesetas,
wanting to keep out of the heat
and watch the deadly goings-on
in perfect comfort.
I was young, of course, and already had a sun
inside of me.
Anyway, what could I possibly have known,
clutching my stub,
of late afternoons in the ring
when the bull's blood ran dark and stained the sand?

Now, many miles and years from Spain,
the shade that creeps towards me
and my place in the sun
is a beautiful dark blade tempered
in the furnace of the sky
and the ticketseller's eyes
have deepened to an absence
above the hollows of his cheeks.
Now, I put everything I have down for Sol,
repeating like one who chants in the temple
sol sol sol
until the sound loses all meaning,
though what I want to say is,
Give me the sun: let my place
any day and all day
be square in those seats
as cheap as breath.

TROUSERS

*"Mandelstam was never able to keep a second
pair of trousers — there was always somebody
whose need was even greater."*
— Nadezhda Mandelstam, *Hope Against Hope*

Only quadrupeds need two pairs of trousers.

Empty trousers hanging in the closet
want to get out and walk.

Let the one-legged man find another
and share with him a single pair of trousers.

I knew a man who hoarded trousers
in anticipation of the day
he would turn into a centipede.

And one pair of trousers for women, too.

Trousers: two hollow columns
atop which sits
an entablature of cloth.
Personal architecture.
The Parthenon of the simple life.

Can you hide extra trousers
by wearing more than one pair at a time?

The saints: those who give away
their only pair.

Like atoms,
the ratio of trousers to people in the universe
remains constant.

For every pair of unused trousers,
a man hangs somewhere from a scaffold
or rafter,
as empty as trousers.

I found this poem
crumpled in a pocket
of the pair of trousers
the darkness, like a clerk
in a store, held out to me
as a sign of my condition
of bareleggedness.

Within trousers, poems;
within poems, trousers.

Heaven: to die
and return to life
as a pair of trousers
always blessed
with its rightful legs.

DEATH AND TELEVISION

Because I chose not to own a television,
Death came to me, before my time, and stayed,
a well-behaved guest, and taught me ease with him.
At fifty, I'd bought myself a country house
tucked into a valley, the south side all windows
framing hills, a horse-pasture, my acreage.
It had the feel of a retreat, strategic,
and even showed its doorless back to the road
in a gesture of privacy, less unfriendly
than simply the perfect place in which to work.
Soon, however, the two primary females
in my life, mother and daughter, campaigned
for me to get a television, bribed
me even: my mother offering to pay
("It's a good way to relax after work"),
my daughter promising more overnights.
Tempted, I almost fell for a salesman's
bargain: "Used. Fifty bucks. Works perfectly."
But some grace saved me from my Two Graces,
their force: maybe already I'd seen the promise
of the house, or heard it: myself, thinking.
Or woods at the windows, as it were, made
the flickering screen seem a violation.
In any case, my non-act was an act,
continuous. A long no that was a longer
yes. And Death must be so totally no
he loves yes more than anything. At least
he said as much, the day he showed up,
friendlier than I expected him to be.
"TV," he said, "doesn't agree with me. And so
I'm pleased to find this place, which feels like home,
if only a temporary one. I'd like
to stay awhile and rest. I'm in no hurry."

(His wish to slow down didn't bother me.)
"I go into house after house where that box
is always on, noisily demanding
everyone's attention like a spoiled child.
It distracts me to the point I can't think straight
and sometimes even forget what, or whom,
I have come for. My hosts ignore me, though all
I'd like's a little talk, some intimacy,
less for my own sake, actually, than theirs."
So we knelt together in the garden,
joking as Death planted only perennials,
and strolled at dusk along the country road
past scattered houses turning dark except
for all their alien lit squares of blue.
Back home, we'd leave every switch unflipped
to sit and watch the rising moon's light throw
itself down in front of us across the
wide carpet, an opera singer playing
Dido on the shore, all grief and abandonment.
We'd sit there, Death and I, savoring
those moments, and listen to the radio —
that verity that blends so well with night,
its music, late news, its strong, clear signals.

CHIAROSCURO

They leave the lights on all over the house.
I come after, turning them off.
I plead and threaten,
but they do not believe
in turning them off.
They believe in lights, everywhere possible
for as long as possible.
They are young,
confident they will return
to this room or that room
and that to turn lights off then on again
is a waste of time,
which they do not have, they say,
though they have lights.
But I have watched and waited
and they do not come back.
The lights will dim and die
before they come back,
though for now,
wherever they've been, there's a light,
and they have been everywhere.

But I do not want the house to seem
to a passerby like a cruise-ship
in mid-ocean, its revel of lights
proclaiming privilege,
defying the vast surround.
I want the house all dark
except for those few places
a person needs to see,
and those places tiny,
a little bedlamp
or table lamp beside a reading chair,

a dim light in the kitchen
where two sit up late talking,
or the faintest of night lights
always there for the restless one
in the still, small hours.
And if I wait long enough,

until everyone else is asleep,
I can sit in a darkened house,
so that the passerby
would have no way of knowing
someone is awake and up inside,
eyes adjusting to what
there is to see
when there is no light,
as more and more of the flood
of darkness slips smoothly
over the rims
of his dilating pupils
and begins
filling him up.